Porsche
911 Carrera, Turbo & RS (964)

Peter Morgan
PMM Books

First published 2003, second edition published 2006, reprinted 2007

ISBN 978 09549990 4 9

Published by PMM Books, an imprint of Peter Morgan Media Ltd.
PO Box 2561, Marlborough, Wiltshire, SN8 1YD, Great Britain.
Telephone: +44 1672 514038
E-mail: sales@pmmbooks.com
Website: www.pmmbooks.com

Ultimate Buyers' Guide
Porsche 911 Carrera, Turbo & RS (964) 1989 to 1994
Contents

Porsche 911 Carrera, Turbo & RS (964)

Introduction

This Ultimate Guide helps you identify and buy the Porsche 911 Carrera, Turbo & RS manufactured between 1989 and 1994. This model family is better known by its Porsche internal number as the type 964.

The 964 was a step change in the 911's long and fascinating development. First introduced in January 1989, it broke ground not only because this first version enjoyed four-wheel drive, but it also dispensed with the classic 911 torsion bar suspension, and replaced them with more modern coil springs. Along with its 250bhp (183kW) 3.6-litre air-cooled engine, standard Anti-lock Braking System and significantly revised styling, the 964 represented an 87 per cent redesign over the previous 911 model – the 911 Carrera 3.2.

The extent of the redesign was no slip of the engineers' pencils. After a long period of growth in the 1980s, Japanese competition was putting the squeeze on the Stuttgart manufacturer.

The 1989 Carrera 4 was followed by a conventional rear wheel drive model and over the remaining life of the 964, there were Turbo, RS and Speedster models alongside the traditional Coupé, Targa and Cabriolet Carreras.

Unfortunately the market was not kind to the 964, and fewer cars sold than the previous Carrera 3.2 or the later 993.

Today, that relative scarcity represents an opportunity to own a 911 that isn't seen all that often.

This Ultimate Buyers' Guide introduces all the 964 types, with facts and figures about performance, detail changes from year to year, production information, special models, options and colours.

In the Buying section, there are tips to help you look at a prospective car, its documentation and information about what makes some cars more desirable than others (by virtue of their colour or the options fitted).

Porsche owners benefit from an extensive official dealer system and in many countries there is an established independent network of specialists.

For impartial information on recommended servicing and maintenance specialists in your area, I would recommend you join your national Porsche club.

The information contained here can't be exhaustive. If you don't feel confident about appraising a particular car, I strongly suggest you seek professional help in the form of a pre-purchase inspection. There are good cars out there, but there are plenty of rogues too!

Peter Morgan
Marlborough, England

Timeline for the 911 Carrera, Turbo & RS (964)

This timeline (and the references used throughout the text) is divided into the automobile industry's model years. This defines a 1991 model as being produced between 1st August 1990 and 31st July 1991.

January 1989

New Porsche 911 Carrera 4 (with 4-wheel drive and in coupe body only) introduced with internal type number 964. 250bhp (183kW), 3.6-litre air-cooled flat-6 engine. facelifted body with coil spring suspension and ABS.

October 1989

Introduction of rear-wheel drive Carrera 2 in Coupé, Targa and Cabriolet models. From January, Tiptronic automatic transmission and on manuals, a dual-mass flywheel. In following March, new 964-based Turbo announced, 3.3-litre single turbo with maximum 320bhp (235kW).

August 1991

Turbo-look bodyshell option for Carrera 2 Coupé and Cabriolet models. Improvements to cylinder head fixings and flywheel. Carrera 2 RS (260bhp, 191kW) introduced from October, with Sport (Lightweight) and Touring models..

August 1992

250bhp (183kW) 911 RS America launched to North American markets, followed by America Roadster (Carrera Cabriolet with Turbo-look). New drive belt breather on distributor. October 1992 sees Turbo engine capacity increased to 3.6-litres, maximum power 360bhp (264kW). Special edition 911 Turbo S with 381bhp (280kW).

February 1993

911 Speedster with raked windscreen, convertible roof and lightweight interior. From March, special edition 911 Celebration for the 911's 30th birthday. 300bhp (220kW) RS 3.8 special edition.

December 1993

911 Carrera 2 Coupé and Targa production ceased. Speedster, Cabriolet and Carrera production continues until beginning of 1994.

911 Carrera Cabriolet (964)

Facts, figures and performance
911 Carrera, Turbo & RS (964)

Bodyshell
Galvanised steel unitary construction, 2 + 2 coupé bodyshell with 2 doors. Hot dip zinc coating with 10 year anti-corrosion warranty. Completely new main structure for bodyshell to accommodate all-wheel drive transmission and coil spring suspension. External body panelling restyled with deformable polyurethane and moving rear spoiler.

New plastic fuel tank capacity: 77 litres (16.94 imp. gallons; 20.3 US gallons). 72Ah battery.

Engine
Normally aspirated engines: Type M64 air-cooled flat-six cylinder engine with larger bore and stroke than previous, lightened crankshaft. Cylinder heads with ceramic exhaust port liners and sodium-filled inlet valves. Chain-driven, single overhead camshaft per side. Aluminium crankcase and cylinder barrels. Dry sump lubrication, Bosch Motronic engine management for ignition and sequential fuel injection. Anti-knock sensing located on middle cylinders

Turbo: Type 930/69 air-cooled flat-six cylinder with bore and stroke as previous 930 model, but with stainless steel head gaskets, larger air-to-air intercooler and three-way catalytic converter

Capacity: 3,600cc; Turbo 3,299cc

Maximum power: Carrera 2/4: 250bhp (187kW) at 6100rpm. Turbo: 320bhp (235kW) at 5,750rpm, RS: 260bhp (194kW) at 6100rpm

Maximum torque: Carrera 2/4: 310Nm (229 lbft) at 4800rpm. Turbo: 450Nm (332lbft) at 4,500rpm. RS: 325Nm (240lbft) at 4800rpm

Transmission
Carrera 4: Type G64/00 five-speed manual gearbox. Carrera 2: Type G50/03 five-speed manual gearbox with revised ratios from earlier model. All-wheel drive cars can transmit up to 31 per cent torque to front wheels. Type A50/01 4-speed Tiptronic automatic transmission optional for Carrera 2. Hydraulic clutch operation and optional limited slip differential for manual cars.

Turbo: Type G50/52 five speed manual transmission with limited slip differential standard. RS: Type G50/10 five-speed manual transmission.

Suspension and steering
Front: Coil spring-over-strut MacPherson design with gas pressure shock absorbers and anti-roll bar. Rear: Coil spring-over-gas pressure shock absorber with semi-trailing arm location. Anti-roll bar. Rack and pinion steering with power assistance.

Brakes, wheels and tyres
Twin-circuit system with brake servo, with Antilock Braking System (ABS) and front to back pressure compensation to maintain balance. Ventilated disc brakes with four-piston calipers all round. 7-spoke 'Club Sport' cast aluminium alloy wheels all round. 6J x 16 with 205/55 tyres front and 8J x 16 with

245/45 tyres rear. 1992 models fitted with Cup Design 91 17-inch wheels.

Performance

Acceleration 0 to 62mph: Carrera 4 and 2: 5.7 seconds; Carrera 2 Tiptronic: 6.6 seconds; Turbo: 5.0 seconds; Turbo S: 4.6 seconds, Turbo 3.6: 4.8 seconds. Carrera RS: 5.3 seconds; Carrera RS 3.8: 4.9 seconds

Maximum speed: Carrera 4 and 2: 162mph; Carrera 2 Tiptronic: 157mph; Turbo: 168mph, Turbo S 180mph, Turbo 3.6: 175mph; Carrera RS: 162mph;

Typical fuel consumption Carrera models (urban and touring): 20 to 25mpg.

Will it fit?

Length: 4250mm (167.3 inches)

Width: 1652mm (65.0 inches); Turbo: 1775mm; RS: 1775mm (69.9 inches)

Height: 1310mm (51.6 inches); Cabriolet: 1320mm (52.0 inches); RS: 1270mm (50.0 inches)

Turning circle: 11.74 metres (3.58 feet)

Kerb weight: Carrera 4: 1450kg; Carrera 2: 1350kg; Turbo: 1470kg; Carrera RS: 1230kg; RS America: 1340kg; Speedster: 1350kg (US model is 1400kg). For Cabriolet add 50kg, for Targa add 50kg.

911 Carrera RS

Porsche 911 Carrera 4 (964)

The 911 Carrera, Turbo and RS (964) story

The 964 is a unique 911 in many ways. Produced at the end of the 1980s in response to an urgent need to update its specification and appeal, it can be viewed as both a success and a failure in equal measure.

Happily for enthusiasts of the marque today, the 964 in all its forms is a wonderful car to drive. It is night and day better than the previous Carrera 3.2. The earlier model feels positively ancient by comparison, but none the less can trace a direct line from the very first production 911 in 1964.

The 964 (the Porsche internal type number given to the project) was fully 87 per cent new – a huge redesign that saw virtually every significant technical aspect of the car changed.

The introduction was a far from orchestrated event. Leaked to the press some one year earlier, the first model to be announced was the Carrera 4, in January 1989. This revolutionary all-wheel drive 911 was a technical *tour de force*, and used engineering expertise earned on the gruelling Paris-Dakar rally and in the Le Mans 24 Hours with the spectacular mid-1980s 959 project.

But four-wheel drive on a 911! This was serious stuff that attacked head-on the old tales that a 911 couldn't – and wouldn't – handle.

The 964's new layout had little of the 959's complex electronics and torque dividing wizardry, but nevertheless, the car's traction was on an altogether more confident level.

Deformable bumpers were the main visual features making the new 964 stand out from earlier 911 models

The handling also benefited from modern coil springs, which replaced the previous torsion bars, while the improved braking equipment was complemented by Bosch Anti-lock Braking System (ABS), the hardware coming from the 928S4.

The air-cooled (of course) flat six-cylinder engine was a significant update from the previous 3.2-litre unit. Capacity increased to a 3.6-litres, with technical highlights including twin spark ignition and anti-knock regulation (controlled by a sophisticated Bosch Motronic engine management).

Maximum power on models in most markets rose from the previous 231bhp (169kW) to fully 250bhp (187kW). Maximum torque increased from 284Nm (210lbft) to 310Nm (229lbft). Innovations included twin-spark ignition controlled by an upgraded Bosch Motronic engine management system (that included anti-knock control).

The first Carrera 4s were only available in Coupé body style. bodywork, initially only in the coupé style, but the classic 911 profile was subjected to a radical (and some would say controversial) facelift. The previous 'impact' bumpers, complete with their organ-style side bellows, were replaced with one-piece deformable polyurethane plastic mouldings. There was also an eye-catching speed-controlled electrically-operated rear spoiler – aimed at improving high speed stability while improving engine bay temperatures.

The rear-wheel drive Carrera 2 was introduced some twelve months after the

The high centre tunnel (to accommodate the all-wheel drive transmission) marks out the interior from earlier 911s

The rear seating is good for young children. The seat backs fold down to make an extra storage area

Carrera 4. And it was worth the wait!

The new model was altogether more sporty in its immediate feel than the earlier Carrera 3.2, thanks to the improved power, suspension, braking and better aerodynamics.

Alongside the Coupé there was now both a Cabriolet and Targa, restoring the three classic body styles of the 911. But the big news in early 1990 was the launch of Tiptronic.

Offered as an option to the conventional manual gearbox, Tiptronic was a 4-speed automatic that also had a manual shift mode.

It would have been inconceivable that Porsche would not have introduced a Turbo version of the new model. Indeed, within the company, the Turbo project had its own project number – 965.

Introduced in December 1990, the new Turbo retained the 3.3-litre 930 engine, uprated from 300bhp to deliver a maximum 320bhp (235kW). The 3.3-Turbo and the later 1993 3.6-litre Turbo remain two of the most exciting 911s you will find – both to look at and to drive.

The early 1990s were a terrible trading period for Porsche and there was a serious risk that the whole business could implode into bankruptcy. This was a time when the product range was offered in any way that was feasible using the existing parts bin. They may not have sold a whole lot, but that period has given us a wealth of different 964 models.

The 1991 Carrera RS was a cracker, derived directly from the successful Carrera Cup racers. It featured all kinds of race-inspired details and a carefully blue-printed engine that was said to give at least 10bhp (7.5kW) more than a standard Carrera 2.

Federal bureaucracy prevented the Carrera RS from being sold in the USA, but two other special 964 models stand out during that time – the RS America and the America Roadster.

In 1993, the 911 reached a significant birthday. The 30th anniversary was celebrated with a 'Celebration' model of the car itself.

A spectacular new Turbo made its debut in January 1993. The 3.6-litre is the last and greatest of the rear-wheel drive, single-turbo 911s. But its time in production can be measured in months rather than the usual Porsche years.

The writing was on the wall for the 964 by 1993. The model had kept Porsche afloat through the most difficult trading period in its history, but to overcome the competition, another design revision was urgently required. The launch of the restyled 993 in December 1993 marked the beginning in a new era of prosperity for Porsche. But as with the 964, not all the new 993 models could be introduced at the same time.

The first 993 model was the Carrera 2, so certain of the 964-bodied Carreras – the 4, Speedster and Cabriolet, plus the spectacular 3.6-litre Turbo, continued in production into 1994.

The 964 formed a vital link between the early, classic 911s and the new generations that would sweep into the world's markets during the later 1990s. In the 964, we began to see the progressive introduction of more electronic driver aids, plus hugely improved ride and handling.

Today, the Carrera 2 and RS models are still considered among the best trackday 911s you can buy. The Turbos deliver the best 'bang for the buck' you can buy in a 911 – because they have none of the refinement of the later twin-turbo models.

If you are looking for top value for touring or everyday use, then the Carrera 4 is unbeatable. And the Cabriolet and Targa offer two very different options for open-air 911 driving.

911 Turbo 3.6 in Black

Model changes year by year

911 Carrera 2 (964) cutaway drawing

Bodyshell

The 964 Coupé's bodyshell represents a major redesign over the previous 911 model – the Carrera 3.2.

Since 1976 all Porsche bodyshells have been dipped in molten zinc and the 964 maintains that industry-leading protection. The 964 family was sold with a ten year warranty against rust perforation (subject to regular checks). This is one reason why many 964s today remain in such good condition.

Accommodating the front differential and drive train of the all-wheel drive system meant significant differences in the shape and size of both the central tunnel in the cabin and in the front compartment. The space at the front of the front compartment is deeper, but the rear is completely filled with the fuel tank. The tank had to be raised to make room for the transmission to the front wheels.

The change to deformable plastic bumpers gives the 911 its most far-reaching appearance change since the introduction of the separate impact-absorbing bumpers in 1974. The latter caused a sensation when they replaced the original 1960s design, and the 964's new polyurethane (PU) items were no less thought-provoking. Squared off plastic sill (rocker panel) extensions complete the 'evolution' look,

The underbody is also completely revised so that it is aerodynamically cleaner. Plastic underbody panels cover the areas between the front wheels and under both the engine and gearbox.

The 964 has an electrically-operated rear spoiler, mounted on the engine cover. The spoiler remains closed while the car is stationary, but when the speed rises above 50mph (80kph), it deploys to provide improved downforce. The moving spoiler also assists engine cooling. As the car slows down, the spoiler retracts at about 7mph (10kph).

The new retractable spoiler is very popular with traditionalists who like the unspoiled early 911 profile. When the 964 was new, the moving spoiler was very suited to the understated '90s.

Other detail changes include improved seals for the windows, which reduce aerodynamic drag, and an updated wind deflector at the front of the sunroof opening.

The Carrera 2 Coupé, the Targa and the Cabriolet trailed the Carrera 4 into production by about a year, but share the same basic bodyshell. The 'wide' bodyshell of the Turbo came in September 1990, but the Turbo-look Carreras didn't appear until a year later.

The only real change to the appearance of the 964 appears with the Turbo's new 'teardrop' style exterior mirrors. These replace the previous 'elephant ear' types on the Carreras for the 1993 model year, which was the last full year of the 964.

The Turbo's trade-mark fixed 'tea-tray' rear spoiler has some revisions from that seen on the previous 930 model and the new PU front bumper has no chin spoiler.

The 1993 models carry the Vehicle Identification Number (VIN) on the left windscreen (A) pillar.

The 'teardrop' mirrors have found their way onto many earlier 964s (as have the later Cup Design 91 wheels and clear turn signal lenses) and make a great update to the overall appearance.

911 Carrera Targa (964). The attraction of the Targa is its combination of practical open air driving and security

Equipment and accessories

The 964 is the first 911 that features sophisticated electronic driver aids and problem warning indicators. The array of warning lights are hidden in the traditional five large round dials. From left to right these display fuel and oil level (in one combi gauge), oil temperature and pressure (in another combi gauge) rpm, speed and on the right, the clock. The headlamp switch is on the lower dash, to the outside of the steering wheel (and ignition key slot).

The new Tiptronic transmission comes with a gear position display in the lower area of the speedometer.

These cars also come with a new onboard trip computer (OBC) that give a range of useful information including fuel consumption, distance to go before refuelling, average speed and outside air temperature.

There is an entirely new electronically-controlled heater system, with a new heater control panel at the centre of the lower dash area. Rotary knobs either side of the traditional position sliders control fan speed and temperature. It is far better than the previous scattered controls.

The only difference on the Turbo's instrumentation is the addition of a boost gauge at the foot of the tachometer (the Turbo was not offered with Tiptronic) and air conditioning is standard.

On the all-wheel drive models, a switch on the centre console controls the differential lock. On the 1990 models, a rocker switch on the upper section of the console allows the rear spoiler to be raised and lowered manually (on early cars this switch is under the spoiler itself).

From this year, all 964s gain a headlamp height adjuster – mounted to the outside of the headlamp switch.

911 Cabriolet with the convertible roof up. Many Cabriolets will have had the roof and plastic rear window replaced after years of exposure

Left-hand drive European 964s gained an airbag from the 1992 model year. Right-hand drive cars followed a year later. This car has tartan cloth inlays to the seats – a special order option by this time

Interior

The 964 retains the 911's evergreen practicality for having usable rear seating. It wouldn't be recommended for four tall adults on a long journey, but pre-teenage children won't have too many complaints in the back. The rear seat backs fold flat for extra storage space.

The interior of the 964 is nearly the same as that in the earlier Carrera 3.2, but with subtle updates to give it a much more modern feel.

The higher transmission tunnel means the manual gear linkage had to be revised from the previous long-throw layout. The 964 shift comes with a shorter travel and a far more precise action.

All the models have a revised rest for the left (clutch) foot, while for the first time, the front compartment bonnet release is on the driver's side on right-hand drive models.

There is a large selection of materials and colours available for the interior. The standard fit is leatherette (grained vinyl) with velour carpets. The optional interiors include the durable full leather, multi-colour studio check or the attractive cloth with in-woven 'Porsche' script.

As well as these, Porsche's 'Special Wishes' department was able to supply interiors to almost any customer fabric and colour sample.

As before, the Turbo comes with a standard full leather for the seats, dash, door cards and centre console trimmings. Its interior could also specified by a customer's special order.

Another special order, this time a full leather Mint Green interior on a Cabriolet. Note the cassette holders behind the handbrake – redundant today in an age of CDs and MP3s!

US cars were fitted with driver and passenger airbags in February 1991. These came to European left-hand drive cars a year later, while right-hand drive cars had a driver's airbag as standard from the 1993 model year. The dash had to be revised to accommodate the passenger airbag installation, and the glovebox moved to a new lower location. The new airbag steering wheel is functional if not elegant, and the large central panel further reduces the view of the lower dash area.

The 1992 models can be identified from earlier versions as they have a time delay on the interior light, and new seat-back releases. The heating system is improved also.

The front compartment carpet upholstery is updated on the 1993 models, gaining three half turn fasteners at the front and Velcro fastenings at the sides, rather than the previous (and fragile) popper studs.

Popular options on the 964 included an electrically operated sunroof, air-conditioning (which was standard in some markets) and heated seats.

From 1993, the air conditioning system was filled with CFC-free refrigerant and these models gain push-button releases for the rear seat backs.

The seats have electric adjustment of the back as standard, which means you still have to operate a lever to move it back and forwards. Full electric operation – with adjustment of the seat height and reach are an option.

The engine bay of this early 964 is dominated by the large, 12-blade cooling fan. The pipes from the air conditioning compressor (arrowed) run over the top of this fan and the central inlet plenum

Engine

The 964's 3.6-litre engine is a significant improvement from the previous 930-based air-cooled flat-six.

The Type M64/01 produces a maximum power of 250bhp (187kW). A larger bore and stroke delivers the extra capacity and along with new, forged pistons with sculpted crowns.

Compression ratio increases from the previous 10.3:1 (for European models) and 9.5:1 (for North American models) to an impressive 11.3:1 for all markets. At the time, Porsche claimed this not only resulted in improved performance, but also reduced fuel consumption, and still allowed the engine to run on premium unleaded (95RON) fuel.

The cylinder heads break new ground in being gasketless – at least until the 1991 models – and feature two sparking plugs per cylinder. The exhaust ports have ceramic port liners to help reduce temperatures in the cylinder heads and improve the efficiency of the catalytic converter (where this was fitted).

The ceramic port liners are so effective that the exhaust valves do not need to be sodium-filled (to help heat transfer). Instead, the inlet valves are sodium filled to help cold starting, lower noise and – by reducing the weight of the valves – allow the engine to run 200rpm faster.

The Nikasil-coated aluminium cylinder barrels are attached to the crankcase as before, by through-bolts. Crucially, these through-bolts employ a new type of sealing ring and seating at the crankcase faces. These seals and the gasketless cylinder heads have proven to be the source of all the 964's serious oil leak problems. It was possible for the seals to be pinched during assembly, causing the frustrating and unsightly leaks, while it proved to be extremely difficult to get the gasketless head/barrel faces to seal properly.

From the 1991 models, the cylinder heads were sealed using an O-ring type metal gasket. This largely solved the cylinder leakage problems and is a well-known retrofit on the earlier engines. These later engines can also be identified by their moulded, black plastic inlet ducting, compared to the cast alloy inlet ducts of the earlier models.

The induction system uses a new two-stage resonant air intake ducting to improve low engine speed torque.

A new, 12-blade cooling fan improves the engine's air cooling, which gives the engine a quite different note to earlier models. A brand new design of camshaft chain tensioner reduces the overall noise still further. The tensioners act on both the driven and driving sides of two (one per cylinder bank) duplex drive chains. The cooling system is also simplified with the deletion of the earlier engine-mounted oil cooler. The oil cooler in the front right-hand wheelarch is larger and fitted with a fan.

The oil in an air-cooled 911 engine serves a double role – to cool as well as lubricate. It is therefore essential to change the oil at the prescribed intervals as it has to work harder than in most other engines.

Dual distribuitors provide the sparks for the twin sparking plugs, with one (the

A pre-'91 964 engine with cast alloy inlet ducts (as indicated by the arrows)

This car is filled with Mobil 1 as used and recommended by Porsche Cars Great Britain Ltd.

A post-'91 engine with the plastic inlet ducts

upper) distributor driven by a toothed belt from the other (itself driven from the crankshaft). The twin-spark system improves the combustion efficiency and allows the ignition timing to be retarded by six degrees, compared to the earlier single-spark 930 engine.

A new Bosch Motronic engine-management system controls the ignition and the all-electronic sequential fuel-injection system. The 964 engine also has anti-knock sensing on the centre cylinders (with the outer cylinders connected by metal straps), to detect pre-detonation.

The 930 engine in the 964-bodied 911 Turbo remains at 3.3-litres, but maximum power increases to 320bhp (235kW) and delivers an impressive 450Nm (332lbft) maximum torque. The 1993 Turbo 3.6 completes the graduation of the Turbo to the new capacity generation.

The Turbo engine uses a resonant air intake with a new exhaust system that has the main silencer on the right side of the engine (with its own tailpipe). The wastegate and outlet from the catalytic converter (fitted for every market) exhausts from the tailpipe on the left.

The turbo's intercooler is fully 50 per cent larger in terms of the air volume it can cool, while the turbocharger itself is larger. At the factory, the boost is set to a standard 0.7 bar (10psi).

The engine's digital motor electronics are upgraded and the result is improved fuel consumption and better exhaust emissions. It is worth noting that full engine management was not yet used on the Turbo (that would come with the 993 version).

Improved engine mountings reduce the amount of vibration that pass into the cabin.

The turbocharger intercooler on the 964 is significantly larger than on the previous 930 model. Note this car has an after-market air filter

Transmission

The first 964-model Carrera 4s use a manual 5-speed gearbox based on the Getrag G50 unit from the Carrera 3.2. The new gearbox is called the G64/00. Compared to the earlier version on the Carrera 3.2, it benefits from revised ratios and an improved shift action.

A differential positioned in the main gearbox splits the torque in the ratio 31 per cent front and 69 per cent rear. A propeller shaft takes the drive forward (from the nose of the gearbox) to a front differential, which in turn drives the front wheels. The differentials can be locked to give improved traction in icy

The basic elements of the Carrera 4's suspension and transmission are revealed in this 1989 photograph

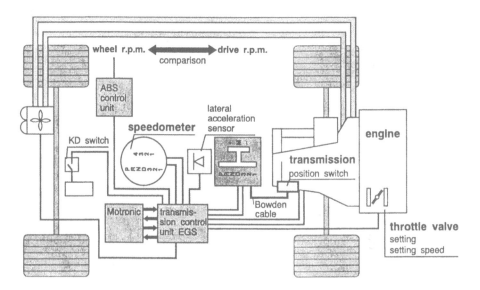

A schematic of the Tiptronic transmission shows how the gearbox is linked to a variety of sensors that detect wheel and vehicle motion. The ABS sensors do more than just detect a skidding wheel!

conditions, using the switch on the centre console. Initially, the Carrera 4 used a conventional single mass flywheel, but for the 1990 model year, a Freudenberg dual-mass flywheel was used on this and the new Carrera 2. The purpose was to improve the smoothness of the engine, with the aim of improving the cabin environment. It was a good idea, in that it aimed to deliver the vibration reduction of a large flywheel at higher rpm, while having the response of a lighter weight flywheel for low rpm.

However, there were problems with the rubber parts used in its construction and for the 1992 model year, 964s began to use a revised dual-mass flywheel design developed by the LUK company.

The Carrera 2 uses the G50/03 gearbox, which is more closely based on the unit in the Carrera 3.2. Of course, it doesn't couple to the centre differential and forward output shaft as fitted to the Carrera 4.

The Tiptronic 4-speed automatic transmission is a major step forward in making the 911 an easier car to live with every day. From the start of Carrera 2 production, it was offered on this model only (not the Carrera 4) as an option to the 5-speed manual gearbox.

Tiptronic offers the choice of fully automatic gearchanges, or clutchless manual ones. Shifts are achieved by tipping (hence the name) the floor-mounted lever back and forth. Moving the lever to the left of the gate offers fully automatic gear selection or the option of selecting gears just as with a traditional automatic gearbox.

The Tiptronic system is electronically controlled to give 'intelligent' operation. It takes engine speed and transmission loading into account when selecting a gear, and accelerometers sense any lateral movement, so that gear changes aren't made during high-speed cornering. The control system prevents selection of the wrong gear for a particular engine or road speed.

Revisions to the Tiptronic system were made to North American cars for the 1992 model year, which included a revised final drive ratio. Keylock and Shiftlock also improved the safeguards on the auto transmission and prevented an incorrect gear being selected. These features were extended to other markets in the following year.

1993 911 Carrera Targa (964) with Cup Design alloys and 'teardrop exterior mirrors. This classic Targa profile is the last of a line that began back in 1966, The 993 would relaunch the model with a completely fresh look

Suspension and steering

Torsion bar suspension has been a defining feature of the 911 since the first prototype saw the light of day back in 1963. Nevertheless, by the 1980s, there was a popular conception that torsion bars were somewhat old-fashioned. In an era of almost universal adoption of coil sprung suspension systems, the old 911's ride and handling needed was considered in serious need of an update. It was also fact that the new all-wheel drive layout proposed for the 964 left little room for the old torsion bars.

Nevertheless, the new suspension layout remains uniquely 911 and its evolution from the original torsion bar system is clear to see.

The front suspension retains the MacPherson strut principle layout, with cast alloy lower control arms and an anti-roll bar. The rear suspension uses the Turbo's cast alloy semi-trailing arms, with a separate 'spring brace' – a cross between the old spring plate and a stabilising radius arm. As with the front axle, sway is also controlled by an anti-roll bar.

The 964 is the first 911 to have power steering – a very useful feature that makes low speed manoeuvering far easier. The power assistance is a conventional system using an engine-driven hydraulic pump (driven off the front of the right side camshaft) driving the steering rack.

The Turbo's springs and dampers are stiffer than the Carreras, with the detail design different on the front axle. Otherwise the layout is the same.

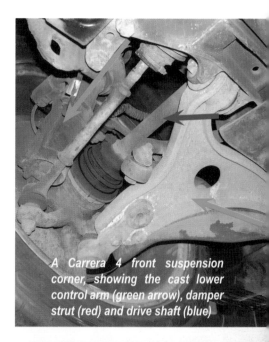

A Carrera 4 front suspension corner, showing the cast lower control arm (green arrow), damper strut (red) and drive shaft (blue)

Rear suspension corner, with semi-trailing arm (green), with damper (red), spring brace (yellow) and drive shaft (blue)

Original 7-spoke alloys as fitted to the early 964s

Cup Design 91 alloys are fitted from the 1992 model year

Cup Design alloys with 9J rims on this 911 Turbo

Brakes, wheels and tyres

The 964 features a brand new braking system, which was developed first on the 928S4. On the Carrera 4, Brembo 4-piston aluminium calipers act on 298mm (front) and 299mm (rear) diameter discs. Until September 1992, the Carrera 2 had 2-piston calipers at the rear. After that both cars use 4-piston calipers all round. The Turbo has cross-drilled discs (as do certain of the special models listed in the following section).

The 3-channel Bosch Antilock Braking System (with sensors on both front wheels and one at the rear) detects wheel locking and reduces the braking pressure until the locking stops.

The first 964s have 16-inch light alloy wheels with seven spokes and a slightly convex face. These simply-styled wheels are called Club Sport or Design 90 and are 6Jx16 at the front and 8Jx16 at the rear. Standard tyres were Bridgestone RE71s which were 205/55ZR16 at the front and 225/50ZR16 at the back.

For the 1992 model year, the 964 received the stylish new Cup Design 91 wheels, which have five spokes and, for the first time, a 17-inch version was available as an option.

The 1991 Turbos use 17-inch Cup Design wheels with 7J and 9J rims and 205/50ZR and 255/45ZR tyres. The 1993 3.6 Turbo comes with very attractive 18-inch, 2-piece Speedline alloys in the same style as the Cup Design.

The spare wheel is a Spacesaver collapsible type that comes with its own 12-volt inflation compressor (that plugs into the cigarette lighter).

Special models

Carrera 2 RS

The Carrera 2 RS was the 1990s answer to the legendary RS 2.7 of 1973. Announced in March 1991, the new car was based on the Carrera 2 but was derived from the 1990 Carrera Cup racing model. The RS followed a well-proven path for lightweight Porsches in that it was stripped of unnecessary equipment to cut the weight down to 1230kg (the standard car was 1450kg).

The RS bodyshell was specially produced and featured seam welding for extra strength and rolled wheel-arch edges to accommodate larger wheels. The front bonnet was made in aluminium, there was no sound proofing and the car used thinner (3mm as opposed to 4.7mm) window glass to reduce the overall weight.

The suspension was solid-bushed, used Bilstein dampers and the anti-roll (sway) bars were adjustable.

The 3.6-litre engine was rechipped to increase the power by 10bhp to a maximum of 260bhp (191kW), while the maximum torque was increased 15Nm to 325Nm (240lbft).

A 7kg lighter, solid (as opposed to dual-mass) flywheel was used, along with solid rubber engine mounts. Only a single V-belt drove the cooling fan.

The suspension was lowered by 40mm, with stiffened shock absorbers and springs to improve the handling. The brakes came from the Turbo. The Cup Design alloys were in magnesium alloy and can be identified by the 'magnesium' and 'Made by SM' cast into the rims.

There were two street versions

911 Carrera 2 RS in the distinctive Rubystone Red. Note deployed rear spoiler and the lower ride height (compare it with the Targa shown on page 26)

of the RS – the Touring and the Sport. The Sport (option M001) was the more extreme version, with a very basic interior and a bodyshell without underbody sealer (it was offered with only a 3-year warranty against rust perforation) and no interior sound insulation.

The specification included a front strut brace, front compartment master switch and the standard 77-litre fuel tank (a larger 92-litre tank was an option). Recaro racing seats were fitted inside, while the rear seats were deleted altogether. Basic door trims, with roll-up windows, and felt carpeting completed the simple accommodation. To reduce weight still further, the Sport's wiring harness was much simplified.

Rather more comfortable was the Touring (option M002), which retained most of the interior trim and accessories of the standard car. This RS kept the Carrera 2's wiring harness and could be fully specified including air conditioning and full sound system. It came with central locking, electric windows, sound proofing and front Sports seats (but no rear seats).

The Club Sport model (also known as Option M003 or N/GT) was a track-ready version of the Sport, complete with welded-in Matter rollover cage, fire extinguisher and Kevlar-shelled Recaro seats with 4-point Schroth harnesses. There was no internal soft trim and the cars came with a sintered metal clutch

A characteristic of all 964RSs is their wild selection of body colours. Among these Rubystone Red and Maritime Blue are the most memorable.

The cabin of the 964 RS is Spartan, with lightweight door cards, roll-up windows and firm bucket-style seats. This car has an aftermarket sports steering wheel

1992-93 RS America

RS America

Made for the North American market from 1992 (where the Carrera 2 RS was not available), the RS America was stripped-out to save weight in much the same way as the C2 RS (although the electric windows and airbags remained). It used a standard 250bhp (183kW) engine and regular production Carrera bodyshell.

At the rear of the car was a fixed whaletail spoiler, and it used the effective M030 sports suspension package. Overall weight was 1345kg.

This was not a race-bred car like the European RS, but was none the less an impressive specification Carrera 2, and makes an excellent basis for a track 911. The RS America sold for about $10,000 less than the standard car, while the European RS was $20,000 more expensive.

Records suggest just 701 RS Americas were sold during 1992 and 1994.

America Roadster

This was special version with an irresistable name for the North American market. This 1992 model was a regular Cabriolet with 2 or 4WD (and optional Tiptronic) in the Turbo's (wide) bodyshell.

The anti-roll bars were stiffened, going from 20mm to 21mm at the front and from 20mm to 22mm (21mm Tiptronic) at the rear.

The America Roadster was powered by the standard 250bhp (183kW) Carrera engine. The convertible roof was electrically-operated and the interior was full leather.

The rear body featured the Carrera's retractable spoiler instead of the Turbo's whaletail (and this does look attractive!).

Some 354 Roadsters (both 2- and 4-wheel drive) were built during the year.

911 Speedster

Carrera 2 Speedster

This 1993 model used Carrera 2 running gear, but had a unique body-style.

Following in the footsteps of the 1989 3.2-litre Speedster, it featured a strongly raked and lower windscreen and a distinctive cover over the simple, manually-operated convertible roof. Much of the interior trim, including Recaro seats, came from the RS, and this was colour-keyed to the external paintwork. The Cup wheels could also be colour-keyed if requested.

Defined as option 503, the Speedster was available in manual or Tiptronic. It was initially only available with the 'narrow' Carrera body, but later was offered as a Turbo-look (and very attractive) wide-body. 936 were built.

Carrera 3.8 RS

Produced as a limited edition to qualify an RSR model for racing in 1993, the RS 3.8 had the wide 911 Turbo bodyshell and is identified by the large bi-plane rear spoiler (see page 34) and attractive 2-piece 18-inch Speedline alloys. The bonnet and doors were aluminium, and it featured a lightweight interior. The engine was based on that of the 3.6-litre 964 unit, but was bored out by 2mm to increase the capacity to 3746cc. That and changes to the Motronic system resulted in a maximum output of 300bhp at 6500rpm.

At 1210kg the RS3.8 is heavier than the Carrera RS M003 version (and perhaps less agile), but the RS3.8 does the 0 to 62mph sprint in just 4.9 seconds and has a top speed of 170mph.

Just 55 street cars were built.

911 Carrera 30 Jahre Celebration

911 Celebration

Just 911 examples of this limited-edition Carrera 4 were built in 1993 to celebrate 30 years of 911 production. The 911 Celebration had the wide Turbo bodyshell (but not that car's suspension or brakes), unique paintwork and a full leather interior.

The cockpit and engine cover featured stylised *911* and *30 Jahre* badging, and there was a limited-edition number stamped onto a plaque on the rear parcel shelf. 911 cars were built.

911 Turbo S

The Turbo S was shown as a study at the 1992 Geneva *Salon* and became a limited edition shortly afterwards. Maximum power from the (M30/69SL) 3.3-litre engine was 381bhp (280kW), while maximum torque was an impressive 490Nm (361lbft).

What made this power count was the lightweight, RS-specification bodyshell, reducing the weight from the standard Turbo's 1470kg (3240lbs) to 1290kg (2844lbs). This included thinner glass and the bonnet and engine cover in carbonfibre. The Turbo S can be identified by its all-plastic whaletail rear spoiler and the openings ahead of the rear wheels. The Turbo S delivered a very firm ride and this was the first time the 'Big Red' brakes were seen and the first use of 18-inch diameter wheels (2-piece Speedline alloys). This model also pioneered what would become the Weissach special colour of Speed Yellow. Just 80 were built.

911 Turbo 3.6 in Guards red

911 Turbo 3.6

Not strictly a special model, but the 1993-4 Turbo 3.6 is here because it is the last of the single-turbo, 'non-electronic' turbos with rear wheel drive. As such it remains to this day one of the most spectacular street 911 Porsche have ever produced.

From this point forward, the later Turbos gained all-wheel drive, twin turbos (for a far smoother power delivery) and sophisticated control electronics.

Presented at the September 1992 Paris Salon, this was a worthy flagship for the Porsche range.

There were actually two Turbo 3.6 models offered in the period 1993-94. The regular model delivered a maximum power of 360bhp (264kW), with peak torque hitting an incredible 520Nm (384lbft). Looks were nearly identical to the earlier 3.3-litre Turbos, except for the 2-piece Cup Design by Speedline wheels on the 3.6. As before a limited slip differential was standard.

The Turbo 3.6 S was built at the end of the 964 Turbo production run and these lightweight cars

1993 911 Carrera Targa Florio,
finished by Porsche Exclusive

were finished Porsche Exclusive. Like the Turbo 3.6, the Turbo S was delivered to all the key markets (Rest of World, Japan and North America).

The M64/50S engine had a maximum power of 385bhp (283kW), allowing the Turbo S to run the 0 to 62mph standing start in just 4.66 seconds – 0.14 seconds faster than the 360bhp model.

Records suggest that of the 1407 Turbo 3.6 and 88 (not confirmed) 3.6S models built from January 1993, 75 were in flat-nose style, with 968-style pop-up headlamps.

911 Carrera Targa Florio

This was a run out special edition of the Targa, built towards the end of the 1993 model year.

The 'Florio' models were finished by Porsche Exclusive – the company's customising department – and included full leather interior with the Porsche crest embossed into the seat backs and several other places. Engine output was unchanged.

The cars were right-hand drive only and can be identified by the 'Florio' logo on the sides of the roll-over hoop.

Production information (1989 to 1994)

Model types and chassis numbers

The following tables are derived from Porsche's own production data and show, year by year, the specific engine and gearbox type used on each model and the chassis and engine number series for that model. This data enables you to identify the actual model year of any car. The chassis number series also show the numbers of each model built.

Table notes

The tables use the following abbreviations: Car = Carrera; Tar = Targa; Cab = Cabriolet; Tip = Tiptronic. All cars are shown by model year (running from August 1 to July 31).

The first models listed for each year are those specified for Germany and Rest of World (RoW) markets, followed by the specific models for the USA (abbreviated to US). Cars for Canada, Switzerland and Austria were largely to USA specification.

The chassis numbers shown are industry standard 17-character Vehicle identification Numbers (VIN). To illustrate what they mean, consider this typical US Carrera 4: WPOAB296LS450001. WPO is the world make code; AB2 is the US VSD code. The first VSD letter is the body type – A, C or D for a coupé, a Cabriolet or a Targa; the second VSD letter is engine/ transmission type – A for two wheel drive, B for four wheel drive; the third VSD digit is the occupant safety system type – 0 for seat belts only, 1 for driver airbag, 2 for driver/passenger airbags. In other markets (like Europe) these three VSD characters are just left ZZZ. Next in the chassis number are the first two digits of the model type (96) followed by a test number (on US models this is usually left blank), the model year letter (K for 1989, L for 1990, etc); S is the plant code (Stuttgart); next is the third digit of the type number (4) and the body/engine code. The last 4 digits are the serial number.

Model	Engine type	Gearbox type	Vehicle Identification Number (VIN)	Engine number
1989 (within Porsche, called the K-series)				
Carrera 4	M64/01	G64/00	WPOZZZ96ZKS400001-2068	62K00051-3176
Carrera 4 US	M64/01	G64/00	WPOAB096_KS450001-1117	62K00051-3176
1990 (L-series)				
Carrera 4	M64/01	G64/00	WPOZZZ96ZLS400001-3957	62L0501-16746
Carrera 4 Targa	M64/01	G64/00	WPOZZZ96ZLS410001-0322	62L0501-16746
Carrera 4 Cabriolet	M64/01	G64/00	WPOZZZ96ZLS420001-0895	62L0501-16746
Carrera 4 US	M64/01	G64/00	WPOAB296_LS450001-1317	62L0501-16746
Carrera 4 Canada	M64/01	G64/00	WPOAB096_LS459001-9080	62L0501-16746
Carrera 4 Tar Canada	M64/01	G64/00	WPOBB096_LS460001-0158	62L0501-16746
Carrera 4 Tar US	M64/01	G64/00	WPOBB096_LS469001-9061	62L0501-16746
Carrera 4 Cab US	M64/01	G64/00	WPOCB296_LS470001-0673	62L0501-16746
Carrera 4 Cab Canada	M64/01	G64/00	WPOCB096_LS479001-9061	62L0501-16746
Carrera 2	M64/01	G50/03	As Carrera 4	62L0501-16746

Carrera 2 Tiptronic	M64/02	A50/01	As Carrera 4	62L50501-1914
Carrera 2 US	M64/01	G50/01	WPOAA296_LS450001-1317	62L0501-16746
Carrera 2 Tiptronic US	M64/02	A50/01	WPOAA296_LS450001-1317	62L50501-1914
Carrera Cup (M001)	M64/01	G64/03	WPOZZZ96ZLS409001-	62L20001-

1991 (M-series)

Carrera 4/2	M64/01	G64/00	WPOZZZ96ZMS400001-7840	62M00001-12930
Carrera 4 US	M64/01	G64/00	WPOAB296_MS410001-1608	62M00001-12930
Carrera 4/2 Targa	M64/01	G64/00	WPOZZZ96ZMS430001-1196	62M00001-12930
Carrera 2 US	M64/01	G50/03	WPOAA296_MS410001-1608	62M00001-12930
Carrera 4/2 Targa US	M64/01	G64/00	WPOBB296_MS440001-0746	62M00001-12930
Carrera 4/2 Cabriolet	M64/01	G64/00	WPOZZZ96ZMS450001-3886	62M00001-12930
Carrera 4/2 Cab US	M64/01	G64/00	WPOCB296_MS460001-2207	62M00001-12930
Carrera 2 Tiptronic	M64/02	A50/01	As Carrera 4	62M50001-5187
Carrera 2 Tiptronic US	M64/02	A50/01	WPOAA296_MS410001-1608	62M50001-5187
Carrera Cup (M001)	M64/01	G64/03	WPOZZZ96ZMS409001-0120	62M20001-120
Turbo	M30/69	G50/52	WPOZZZ96ZMS470001-2298	61M00001-3327
Turbo US	M30/69	G50/52	WPOAA296_MS480001-674	61M00001-3327

1992 (N-series)

Carrera 4	M64/01	G64/00	WPOZZZ96ZNS400001-4844	62N00501-08240
Carrera 4 US	M64/01	G64/00	WPOAB296_NS420001-0715	62N00501-08240
Carrera 4 Targa	M64/01	G64/00	WPOZZZ96ZNS430001-0597	62N00501-08240
Carrera 4 Targa US	M64/01	G64/00	WPOBB296_NS440001-0211	62N00501-08240
Carrera 4 Cabriolet	M64/01	G64.00	WPOZZZ96ZNS450001-2885	62N00501-08240
Carrera 4 Cab US	M64/01	G64/00	WPOCB296_NS460001-0992	62N00501-08240
Carrera 2	M64/01	G64/00	WPOZZZ96ZNS400001-4884	62N00501-08240
Carrera 2 Tiptronic	M64/02	A50/02	As Carrera 4	62N50501-52864
Carrera 2 Tiptronic US	M64/02	A50/03	WPOAA296_NS420001-0715	62N50501-52864
Carrera 2 RS (inc M002)	M64/03	G50/10	WPOZZZ96ZNS490001-2051	62N80001-938
Carrera 2 RS (M003)	M64/03	G50/10	WPOZZZ96ZNS499001-290	62N80001-938
Carrera Cup	M64/03	G50/10	WPOZZZ96ZNS498001-113	62N80001-938
Carrera 2 RS America	M64/01	G50/05	WPOAA296_PS418001-8298	62N00501-08240
Turbo	M30/69	G50/52	WPOZZZ96ZNS470001-836	61N00501-01605
Turbo US	M30/69	G50/52	WPOAA296_NS480001-309	61N00501-01605
Turbo S	M30/69	G50/52	WPOZZZ96ZPS479001-081	61N00501-01605

1993 (P series)

Carrera 4	M64/01	G64/00	WPOZZZ96ZPS400001-3249	62P00501-06490
Carrera 4 US	M64/01	G64/00	WPOAB296_PS420001-0520	62P00501-06490
Carrera 4 US (718)	M64/01	G64/00	WPOAB296_RS420001-0280	62P00501-06490
Carrera 4 Targa	M64/01	G64/00	WPOZZZ96ZPS430001-0419	62P00501-06490
Carrera 4 Targa US	M64/01	G64/00	WPOBB296_PS440001-0137	62P00501-06490
Carrera 4 Targa US (718)	M64/01	G64/00	WPOBB296_RS440001-00081	62P00501-06490

Carrera 4 Cabriolet	M64/01	G64/00	WPOZZZ96ZPS450001-1414	62P00501-06490
Carrera 4 Cab US	M64/01	G64/00	WPOCB296_PS460001-0600	62P00501-06490
Carrera 4 Cab US (718)	M64/01	G64/00	WPOCB296_RS460001-0138	62P00501-06490
Carrera 2	M64/01	G50/03	WPOZZZ96ZPS400001-3249	62P00501-06490
Carrera 2 US	M64/01	G50/05	WPOAA296_PS420001-0520	62P00501-06490
Carrera 2 Tiptronic	M64/02	A50/02	As Carrera 4	62P50501-1876
Carrera 2 Tiptronic US	M64/02	A50/03	As Carrera 4 US	62P50501-1876
Carrera 2 RS America	M64/01	G50/05	WPOAA296_PS418001-0450	62P00501-06490
Carrera 2 RS Amer (718)	M64/01	G50/05	WPOAA296_RS418001-068	62P00501-06490
Speedster	M64/01	G50/03	WPOZZZ96ZRS455001-509	62P00501-06490
Speedster US	M64/01	G50/05	WPOCA296_RS465001-427	62P00501-06490
Carrera RS 3.8 (M004)	M64/04	G50/10	WPOZZZ96ZPS497061-129	62P85001-662
Carrera RSR 3.8	M64/04	G50/10	WPOZZZ96ZPS496060-104	62P85001-662
Carrera Cup	M64/	G50/10	WPOZZZ96ZPS498001-015	62P80501-515
Turbo 3.6 (from 1/93)	M64/50	G50/52	WPOZZZ96ZPS470001-650	61P00001-1614
Turbo US (from 1/93)	M64/50	G50/52	WPOAA296_RS480001-288	61P00001-1614

1994 (R-series)

Carrera 4	M64/01	G64/00	WPOZZZ96ZRS400001-0505	62R00001-1617*
Carrera 4 US	M64/01	G64/00	WPOAB296_RS420001-0456	62R00001-1617*
Carrera 2	M64/01	G50/03	WPOZZZ96ZRS400001-0505	62R00001-1617*
Carrera 2 US	M64/01	G50/05	WPOAA296_RS420001-0456	62R00001-1617*
Carrera 2/4Cabriolet	M64/01	G50/G64	WPOZZZ96ZRS450001-0315	62R00001-1617*
Carrera 2/4 Cabriolet US	M64/01	G50/G64	WPOCB296_RS460001-0283	62R00001-1617*
Carrera RS America	M64/01	G50/05	WPOAA296_RNS419001-144	62R00001-1617*
Speedster	M64/01	G50/03	WPOZZZ96ZRS455001-5581	62R00001-1617*
Speedster US	M64/01	G50/05	WPOCA296RS465001-5469	62R00001-1617*
Turbo	M64/69	G50/52	WPOZZZ96ZRS470001-471	61R00001-01301
Turbo US	M64/69	G50/52	WPOAC296_RS480001-466	61R00001 01301

*Engine series shown is for manual gearbox cars only. Tiptronic engines manufactured were in the range 62R50001-1857. The first 60 serial numbers of each VIN is usually reserved for internal use.

North American cars built after May 1993 were given the 1994 model year designator 'R', as an inducement to boost flagging sales. These models are shown with option code M718. They are easily identified by the 'R' letter in the 10th digit position of the chassis number.

The manual gearbox for the Carrera 4 was the same for all markets except Switzerland where lower ratios were fitted on the top two gears to reduce acoustic noise levels. That gearbox is known as G64/01. For the Swiss Carrera 2 models, the gearbox became G50/02. Where a limited slip differential was fitted to the Carrera 2, this can be identified in the Service & Maintenance Book as G50/03 (G50/04 in Switzerland). For 1991, Taiwan cars received gearbox G64/02

The data on Carrera RS, Carrera RSR, Carrera RS 3.8 etc is compiled from personal research in factory records, and the figures given carry no official backing or verification..

The 3.3-litre 911 Turbo S was a lightweight sports version of the regular Turbo. The Turbo S was the first Porsche to feature 'Big Red' Brembo brake calipers and the 18-inch Speedline alloys. Note the race credit on the lower side trims for the US IMSA Supercar Championship

Year by year body colours and interior choices

This section lists the colour choices and fabrics available from year to year. The colour code sticker on a 964 can be found on the left-side inner wing (as you sit in the car) within the front compartment, near the battery. You will need to detach the sidewall carpet (as shown earlier in this guide) to see this

1989

Standard external body colours

Guards Red (80K), Black (700), Linen Grey (60M), Apricot Beige (548), Murano Green (22C), Grand Prix White (908), Dark Blue (347).

Special colours

Forest Green met. (22E), Cognac Brown met. (40L), Coral met. (81K), Baltic Blue met. (37B), Slate Grey met. (22D), Velvet Red met. (81L), Diamond Blue met. (697), Linen Grey met. (550), Silver met. (980), Stone Grey met. (693).

Fabrics

Leatherettes in Linen Grey (4WX), Burgundy (3MK), Blue (1KX), Mahogany (1MX), Black (43S), Cashmire Beige (7RT).
Leathers in Burgundy (7LD), Mahogany (2LX), Venetian Blue (7KC), Black (1AJ), Blue (7JX), Cashmire Beige (2WH), Velvet Red (4MT), Linen Grey (7VX), Silk Grey (5VT), Slate Grey (2WT), Caramel (4UC). Pin stripe velours in Linen Grey/White (4WJ), Black/White (7BN), Mahogany/White (6LN), Blue/White (8GJ), Burgundy/White (1MJ), Cashmire-Beige/White (4TN). Multi-colour Studio Check in Black (2VV), Mahogany (8XV), Blue (9JV), Burgundy (1MV), Linen Grey (6UV), Cashmire Beige (5TC). Fabric with in-woven diagonal 'Porsche' script in Black (2CZ), Cashmire-Beige (7TH), Mahogany (4MR), Blue, (6HZ), Burgundy (5LZ), Linen Grey (5WZ).

Cabriolet roof material

Black, Mahogany, Blue and Burgundy.
Carpets: Silk velours in Mahogany (5MF), Blue (4KV), Linen Grey (2XF), Burgundy (8MD), Black (5FV), Slate Grey (3WT), Cashmire Beige (8UT), Velvet Red (9MT), Silk Grey (7VT), Caramel (5UM), Venetian Blue (3KM).

1990

External colours

As 1989 plus Marine Blue met. (35V).
Special colours for Carrera 4 and 2, announced 10/89: Satin Blue met., Oak Green met., Venetian Blue met., Violet Blue met., Cassis Red met., Tahoe Blue met., Granite Green met., Turquoise met., Lagoon Green met., Zermatt Silver met..
Fabrics and carpets: All as 1989.

1991

External colours

Guards Red (80K), Black (700), Rubystone Red (82N), Maritime Blue (38B), Grand Prix White (908), Signal Green (22S), Mint Green (22R).
Special colours: Cobalt Blue met. (37U), Oak Green met. (22L), Polar Silver met. (92E), Slate Grey met. (22D), Black met. (738), Horizon Blue met. (37X), Midnight Blue met. (37W), Coral Red met. (82H), Amethyst met. (38A), Amazon Green met. (37Z).
For Carrera 2 RS: Amethyst met., Rubystone Red, Black, Maritime Blue, Midnight Blue met., Guards Red, Grand Prix White, Polar Silver met..

Fabrics

Leatherettes in Classic Grey (5WH), Cobalt Blue (5ZF), Light Grey (3ZT), Magenta (9WX), Black (43S), Cashmire Beige (7RT). Leathers in Classic Grey (6XL), Light Grey (8ZL), Black (8YR), Cobalt Blue (9YL), Cashmire Beige (4YU), Magenta (6YL), Sherwood Green (J25), Carrara Grey (D35), Matador Red (M05). Multi-colour Studio

Check in Black (2VV), Classic Grey (9WT), Cobalt Blue (9YD), Magenta (1MV), Light Grey (6UV), Cashmire Beige (5TC). Fabric with in-woven diagonal 'Porsche' script in Black (2CZ), Cashmire-Beige (7TH), Light Grey (7TH), Classic Grey (6WC), Cobalt Blue (7ZK), Magenta (9YC).
Carpets: Silk velours in Classic Grey (4XR), Light Grey (6YR), Magenta (8WZ), Cobalt Blue (4ZN), Black (5FV), Matador Red (M33), Cashmire Beige (8UT), Carrara Grey (D13), Sherwood Green (J23).

1992
External colours
Standard colours: Black (A1), Guards Red (G1), Grand Prix White (P5), Rubystone Red (G4), Maritime Blue (F2), Signal Green (M1), Mint Green (N4).
Metallic colours: Blue met. (Z8), Amazon Green met. (N7), Amethyst met. (F9), Slate Grey met. (Q9), Horizon Blue met. (F4), Coral Red met. (G7), Oak Green met. (N9), Cobalt Blue met. (F6), Midnight Blue met. (F8), Polar Silver met. (A8).
Special colours: Satin Blue met. (50) Marine Blue met. (56), Cassis Red met. (52), Violet Blue met. (57), Granite Green met. (53), Tahoe Blue met. Lagoon Green met. (54), Turquoise met. (59), Zermatt Silver met. (55).
Special colours for Turbo-look
Raspberry Red met. (with red interior), Wimbledon Green met. (green interior), Lavender Blue met.(grey interior).
Fabrics
Multi-colour Studio Check in Blue, Light Grey, Cashmire Beige, Classic Grey, Light Grey, Cobalt Blue. Porsche fabrics in same colours.
Leather in Black, Light Grey, Cashmire Beige, Light Grey, Cobalt Blue.

Custom leather in Matador Red, Carrara Grey, Sherwood Green.
Cabriolet roof material
Black, Dark Blue, Cobalt Blue and Magenta.

1993
External colours
As 1992 excluding Rubystone Red. Specials are as 1992 excluding Coral Red metallic, but including Violet Blue met. (57), Wimbledon Green met. (B5) and Raspberry Red met. (A7), but also including, from early 1993, Speed Yellow.
Fabrics
Interiors as 1992: Cabriolet roof materials as 1992, but incl. Classic Grey.

Options
This is a list of factory options for the 964 (and does not claim to be exhaustive). In many markets, certain of these options were offered as part of the standard package. The options fitted to a car (other than those market-specific options) can be found on the vehicle identification label (VIL), found under the bonnet or in the vehicle's factory Service and Maintenance booklet. Note that all the options start with the letter M.

M18 Sport steering wheel with elevated hub
M26 Activated charcoal canister
M030 Sport suspension for Carrera 2 (1992/3)
M70 Tonneau cover – Cabriolet
M103 Adjustment of shock absorber strut
M139 Seat heating – left
M154 Control unit for improved emissions
M156 Quieter silencer
M185 Automatic two point rear seat belts
M186 Manual rear seat belts
M187 Asymmetric headlamps
M195 Prepared for cellular telephone
M218 Licence brackets, front and rear
M220 Locking differential 40 per cent
M240 Version for countries with inferior fuel

M261 Passenger external mirror, flat glass
M286 High intensity windshield washer
M288 Headlight washer
M326 Radio Blaupunkt Berlin
M327 Radio Blaupunkt Koln
M328 Radio Blaupunkt Bremen
M328 Radio Blaupunkt Symphony
M329,30 Radio Blaupunkt Toronto
M335 Automatic 3 point rear seat belts
M340 Seat heating – right
M351 "Porsche CR stereo" radio/cassette Type DE, manual antenna, loudspeakers.
M379,80 Series seat, electric vertical adjustment, left, right.
M383,7 Sports seats, electric vertical adjustment, left, right
M389 "Porsche CR stereo US" radio/cassette, manual antenna, loudspeakers.
M391 Stone guard decal
M399 Air conditioning without front condensor
M407 Rear seats with static belts
M409 Sport leather seats, left, right
M410 Sport seats in leatherette/cloth, left, right
M454 Cruise control
M463 Clear windshield
M464 Without compressor and tyre pressure gauge
M467 External drivers mirror, convex
M483 Right hand drive
M492 H4 headlights for left hand traffic
M498 Without rear model designation
M503 Speedster variant of Cabriolet
M528 Passenger side external door mirror, convex
M533 Alarm system
M562 Airbags, driver and passenger sides 1990-on models
M564 Without airbag
M565 Safety steering wheel in leather, 380 mm diameter
M573 Air conditioning
M577 Heated and tinted windshield
M602 Third brake light - top of rear screen
M605 Vertical headlight adjustment

M630 Police equipment
M659 On board computer
M686 Radio Blaupunkt Ludwigsburg
M688 Radio Blaupunkt, Boston
M690 CD player CD10 with radio
M691 CD player CD02 from 1989, with radio
M980 Seat covering in raff leather
M981 All leather lining
M986 Partial leather lining

Country codes

Porsche builds cars for many different markets. With demand high for the various 993 models, cars that were originally built for other countries are often imported from outside the receiving country's official network. However, the standard specification for one country may not be the same as another and key options or roadworthiness compliance requirements can often be omitted. Porsche give each car a destination country code and it is easy to identify this. The best residual values will always be achieved by cars with the same country code as where you live, although whether that car was imported through official or unofficial channels appears to be unimportant.

Some of the key country codes are listed below

C00 Germany, C02 Rest of USA, C03 California, C05 France, C07 Italy, C08 Japan (LHD), C09 Sweden, C10 Switzerland, C11 Austria, C12 Denmark, C13 Finland, C15 Hong Kong, C16 GB, C17 British service personnel stationed in Germany, C18 Japan (RHD), C19 Luxemburg, C20 Holland, C21 Norway, C22 Belgium, C23 Australia, C24 New Zealand, C26 South Africa, C27 Spain, C28 Greece, C36 Canada, C98 Non-specific RHD

Buying a used 964

There are some basic rules that apply to buying any used car. You won't remember all these words when you go to see cars, but the most important rule is not to buy on impulse.

If you like a car, but you don't have the time to do a thorough check or doing it bores you, get an expert to do that. It could save you thousands on either repair bills or when you come to sell it.

If you have to put a holding deposit on a car you like, keep it as small as possible. Many dealers will refuse to refund a deposit if you change your mind.

This section will go into greater detail on the areas of the car that must be checked out before sale, to lessen the risk of heartbreak later on. We'll start with what to look for in the car's documentation.

Documentation

The importance of proper documentation cannot be stressed enough.

The starting point is that the car is registered in the seller's name and that the statutory registration documents are available and in order. Be extra cautious if you are told the registration document is 'away' or in transit.

The registration documents should show the car's Vehicle Identification Number (VIN), or chassis number. Check this number against the expected series for the declared model year.

If you are looking for one of the higher performance models, note the differences in the VIN between a regular Carrera and (say) a Turbo or RS. In these cases the engine number on the car should also be

VIL as found under the bonnet of a 964. The 'N' at the tenth digit marks this as a 1992 model. The 'C00' in the first line of the option codes shows the car to be to German specification

checked against the listings for that model. It isn't unknown for an RS to have had a regular Carrera engine dropped in when nobody was looking, or for both these higher performance models to be reshelled.

The VIN appears on the Vehicle Identification Label (VIL), which can be found early in the Guarantee & Maintenance booklet and under the bonnet. The same page of the Guarantee & Maintenance booklet will also show the supplying dealer and the date of delivery to the first customer.

It is not unknown for the VIL to be missing from the service booklet. This can be because the VIL was mislaid at the time of delivery. However, it is worth remembering that in the worst case, a missing VIL may indicate a completely duplicated (and hence false) service history.

If the VIL is missing from under the bonnet, then it suggests the bonnet has been replaced (and therefore you should be ready to find other damage repairs).

If both the G&M VIL and the bonnet VIL are missing, this means the vehicle's identity cannot be verified. At worst, it could mean the car has a false identity. At best, the price should reflect the uncertainty in the identity.

The car's options are listed at the foot of the VIL, beginning with the country code (see page 42). The country code allows you to verify the country of origin of the car.

Since all 964s are now more than 10 years old, the original Porsche warranty against rust will have expired,. Nevertheless, if the Maintenance book shows an early record of servicing within the official network, it may indicate that the bodyshell was kept in top condition in the first part of the car's life.

That said, there is a very good financial argument for having a recognised Porsche specialist take over the servicing after about 3 years or 40,000 miles and many 964s will have a service history within the independent

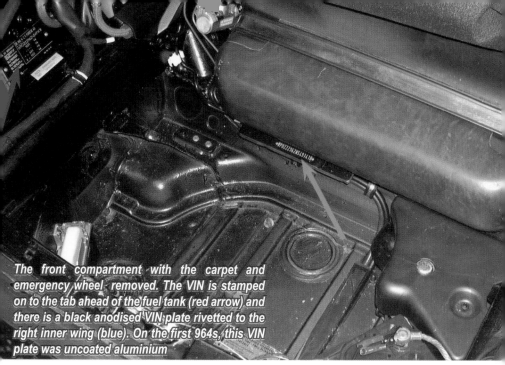

The front compartment with the carpet and emergency wheel removed. The VIN is stamped on to the tab ahead of the fuel tank (red arrow) and there is a black anodised VIN plate rivetted to the right inner wing (blue). On the first 964s, this VIN plate was uncoated aluminium

network. Whichever organisation has stamped the book, the record also provides the first evidence of the car's actual mileage. The key aspect when assessing the service record is that the servicing is regular – ideally every year (whatever the mileage).

The service stamps alone are not enough to fully consolidate the mileage on the odometer (because both can be falsified by the unscrupulous). Ideally there will be a sheaf of bills with the car to support the servicing, and many of these bills will show the car's registration number and mileage at the time of the work. The bills will also help determine whether wear and tear items like the clutch, brake discs and pads, battery and tyres have been replaced recently.

Of course, unattractive bills will always generally be 'mislaid' from a car's records, and that's why there is no substitute for a thorough inspection of the car itself.

In the UK, after three years every car must pass an annual roadworthiness test (called the MoT, after the Ministry of Transport that came up with the legislation). There are many similar annual roadworthiness checks in other parts of the world. An unbroken run of such checks to the current date will also support the odometer reading.

It is not unusual for cars to have had speedometers replaced (particularly if the car is an import), but it should be possible to work out the accumulated mileage from the documents provided.

Without exception, if there are serious inconsistencies in the mileage record, you should ignore the car.

In the UK you can check whether a UK-registered car has any outstanding finance, has been declared a write-off or has a Police history by going onto the HPI website (www.hpicheck.com).

Poorly replaced sill trim seals are a giveaway for a budget repair

Large gap between this Targa roof seal and the top of the windscreen probably means it will leak

Targa roof removed from the car and folded. Always check the inner and outer skins, plus the beading for splits

Bodyshell

The VIN is stamped onto the Vehicle Identification Label (VIL) that is found under the bonnet (and in the Guarantee & Maintenance booklet). It is a self-adhesive label and ideally should not be missing or altered in any way. This number should agree with the number stamped on to a tab welded to the bodyshell, just under the front of the fuel tank (found under the carpet in the front compartment). 1993 and later model 964s also have the VIN shown on a tab on the left-side windscreen pillar

These numbers should all agree with each other and match the number shown in the vehicle's official documentation.

Using the chassis number information from the car and the tables reproduced in this guide, check that the car is from the model year series being claimed by the seller. This is particularly important when say, discovering whether the car is a '90 model or an improved '91 model.

Externally, new paint can often be given away by poor finish, overspray on the flexible trim or a raised paint line along a seam. Look carefully along the flanks of the body, looking for panel misfits, poor surface finish or dents in the doors (from car park contacts).

Quite often, small bodywork repairs will have been carried out by a mobile paint restoration service. The quality of workmanship of these mobile services is very mixed and the reworked area can often look worse than before.

There is no substitute for having external bodywork restoration or repairs performed by a fixed base, top quality paintshop. As well as colour mismatches, look also for an 'orange peel' or feathered finish and differing gaps around the doors, bonnet and engine cover.

Evidence of major crash repairs will often show on the internal bodyshell longitudinals, both in the front compartment and in the engine bay. Unlike the 993, the paint finish in the 964's front compartment is usually good, with no half-painted or 'missed' areas. Look for poor workmanship, untidy wiring and missing paint code label or VIN plate to suggest the area has been reworked. With the engine cover open, check the spot-welding marks in each side gutter. They should be the same appearance on a car with its original wings.

The inspection will also establish if the car is in its original body colour (check the label on the right-side of the front compartment) or is a reshell (without the VIN appearing on the tab below the fuel tank). Without exception I would advise against buying any such cars.

Corrosion shouldn't generally be a problem with the 964 as the bodyshell is manufactured from zinc-dipped steel. Nevertheless, accident repairs often break the protective coating and the finish can often be blistered by attack from high intensity screen wash or rubbing by screen sealing strips.

These rust blisters are unsightly, but they can be cleaned up by a proper paintshop. You may also find that the black anodising on the door window frames and the side windows has become partly blistered. This is the result of corrosion of the underlying aluminium. This can also be fixed, but it may be outside the scope of your local bodyshop. Consult a service specialist for advice on how to refinish the anodising.

The front and rear bumpers are deformable polyurethane and are designed to withstand

Deep scratches like this will mean a repaint of the whole front bumper

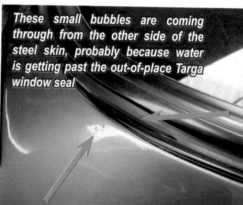

These small bubbles are coming through from the other side of the steel skin, probably because water is getting past the out-of-place Targa window seal

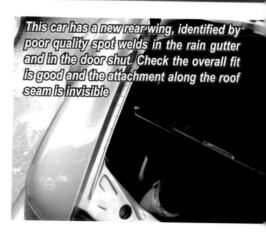

This car has a new rear wing, identified by poor quality spot welds in the rain gutter and in the door shut. Check the overall fit is good and the attachment along the roof seam is invisible

White isn't as popular a colour as it was in the early 1990s

low speed impacts. There should be no splits or cracks in their surfaces – if there are it suggests the bump has been harder than you might wish. The small air outlets ahead of the front wheels can be easily damaged on high kerbs and gate centre-posts can wreak havoc on the smooth undertray.

Another sign of a repair can be gaps in the plastic sill seals. If there is a large seal gap in the area just behind the door opening, then its an indication that the sill trims have been off for a repaint on that side.

Each door should close easily and without having to slam it. If there is a significant difference in the closing effort, it may suggest the bodyshell is twisted or the door has been poorly replaced after repairs.

Stone chips (they are a fact of life these days) can seriously degrade the value of a car. Check the external mirrors and the areas in front of the rear wheelarches for pitting. Stone guards – the adhesive-backed clear plastic decals ahead of the rear wheelarches – should not be painted over.

Stone chip damage is a good bargaining point when buying, since a professional repaint of the affected panels is an excellent way of freshening up the looks – and value – once you own it.

When buying a pre-owned car, you often don't get much choice when it comes to colour. But that said, the right colour can make a big difference to a car's desirability, and its instant 'wow' factor. And if you are impressed with the colour when you buy the car, then in turn, when you come to sell it later, so will be your prospective buyer.

For the 964, the popular colours are Silver, the dark blues and grey metallics. Guards red (still) has its own fan club, but sadly, white and green always seem to linger longer in the showrooms.

When looking at a special model (particularly the Carrera RS, be very aware of the particular bodyshell modifications these cars were given (for instance the seam-welded shell, rolled wheelarch edges, aluminium bonnet and thin-gauge glass). For more information on these differences, go to page 29.

Cabriolet roofs need careful consideration. Old roofs are prone to damage at the sides, just above the rear edge of the side windows. There's a dowel pin either side in the mechanism underneath, that if badly adjusted, will work through the material. Check the underlying material for Duck tape patches!

The plastic rear window is prone to milkiness and general surface degredation. Replacement of the roof or the window is not cheap, and I would not recommend some of the after-market budget replacements (as they often don't fit properly or degrade faster than the Porsche original.

The Targa roof material is prone to splitting where it folds, so check the outer and inner skins carefully. Check the weather seals around the windscreen top and around the front edge of the roll-over hoop. If these seals are worn, water can find its way into the cabin, soak the carpets and rot them.

A carefully-owned Targa will also have no scratching or marking of the black roll-over hoop finish. There should also be two toggles in the glovebox to release the front locks at the top of the windscreen.

Under the car, look for signs of grounding under the front bumper and distortion of the jacking points. The latter can be damaged by off-road excursions and render the car unliftable with its own jack.

Poor jacking on workshop elevators or lifts can also remove the sealer in the corners of the underbody nearest the wheels and pro-mote corrosion.

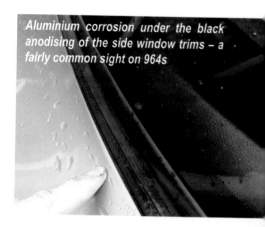

Aluminium corrosion under the black anodising of the side window trims – a fairly common sight on 964s

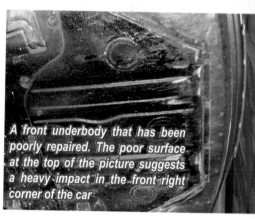

A front underbody that has been poorly repaired. The poor surface at the top of the picture suggests a heavy impact in the front right corner of the car

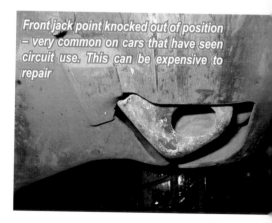

Front jack point knocked out of position – very common on cars that have seen circuit use. This can be expensive to repair

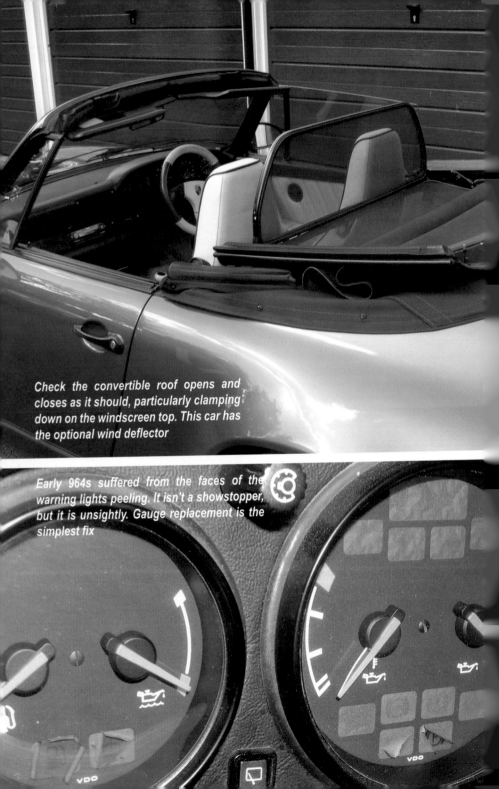

Check the convertible roof opens and closes as it should, particularly clamping down on the windscreen top. This car has the optional wind deflector

Early 964s suffered from the faces of the warning lights peeling. It isn't a showstopper, but it is unsightly. Gauge replacement is the simplest fix

Equipment, trim and accessories

Check the windscreen carefully for unsightly signs of delaminating (where the plastic film inner separates from the glass), usually at the edges. More important to roadworthiness are heavy chips and cracks in the glass. If a crack attracts your attention and is any more than 1-2mm in diameter, then the windscreen it may need repair with resin or even replacement. It's my opinion that no matter how good the repair resins are claimed to be, they are only a temporary fix.

A good 964 can be ruined by poor installation of aftermarket electrical equipment. This equipment can be either a secondary alarm, improved sound system. There shouldn't be a 'rat's nest' of wiring under the dash or crammed into the fuse panel (found at the back of the front compartment on the right side of the car).

Always check that all the electrical equipment and accessories work as designed, because tracing some faults can work out expensive. On some early 964s the warning lights in the gauges suffered from peeling faces (due to the heat generated behind them). Replacement used parts may be the most cost-effective solution.

Check the clock works, that the cigarette lighter socket has power (because you want to be able to inflate that emergency spare wheel!) and that the windows work. With the ignition on, the electrically-operated rear spoiler should also deploy when the centre console-mounted switch (under the engine cover on early cars) is pressed. On the move, the spoiler deploys automatically at 50mph and retracts at around 7mph.

The heating system works by passing fresh air over the hot exhaust pipes. This

Most original convertible roofs will be very time worn by now. Check for tears and splits, and that the plastic rear window is transparent and undamaged

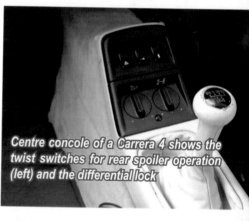

Centre concole of a Carrera 4 shows the twist switches for rear spoiler operation (left) and the differential lock

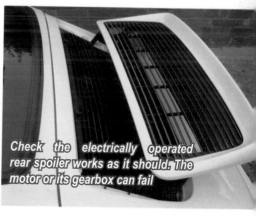

Check the electrically operated rear spoiler works as it should. The motor or its gearbox can fail

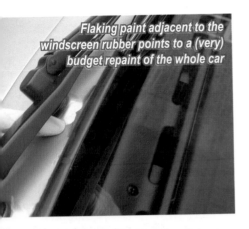

Flaking paint adjacent to the windscreen rubber points to a (very) budget repaint of the whole car

A look into the area ahead of the door hinge post reveals that this Midnight Blue car was once Guards Red

The heater control panel is completely obscured from the driving seat, so you'll develop a very good feel for the controls!

warmed air is then ducted into the cabin, and is automatically mixed with cool air along the way to ensure the correct temperature.

Test the heater operation when the engine is warm. With the fan output set (on the dash panel) to medium speed, turn the temperature control to hot. When the delivery is warm, turn the dial to minimum. The change in output should be felt immediately. Then push the air conditioning 'snowflake' button and within five seconds you should feel a definitely chilled output.

Both a noisy fan or faulty heater control panel can be relatively expensive to replace.

Check that the external mirrors move in two planes and that the mirror heaters work (they will be warm to the touch). Run each window up and down – the little-used passenger side unit may be slow, but if it doesn't work, a new motor may be required. Faults like these may be traceable to nothing more than a loose or corroded connection, but non-working or faulty items can give you more bargaining power.

Check the central locking works (and on the remote key fob if provided). While outside the car, check all the headlamp and other lenses for chipping. The turn signal and rear reflector lenses are prone to internal condensation or cracks. Of course, check all the lights work as they should.

If the car is a left-hand drive import (into the UK, say), ensure it has been changed over to right-hand drive lighting and that there is an MPH speedometer and odometer. There should be a bill or some documentation underwriting the odometer reading (or the old speedo itelf) at the point the change out was made.

Interior

Accidental damage and wear and tear are the major problems on upholstery that will have seen many years of continuous use. The best buys are those cars with tough, dark-coloured leather interiors. The lighter colours look great when clean, but both bolsters and the seat beading have a reputation for wear. The important aspect is to remember what is an expected level of wear and tear on a car of this age – and don't expect showroom condition!

On a general level, look first for rips and tears in the seats (particularly the driver's side bolster and the seat backs). A common damage sign is when unusual objects have been loaded into the car, marking the plastic trim or scraping the upholstery. The individual carpet pieces (these 911s didn't have sculpted carpets) can also take a beating. Because they can move around quite easily, the edges can wear and the lighter colours will stain over the years. There should be no dampness or wetness under the carpets, next to the floor. A water leak usually suggests poor sunroof or door seals.

Check the dash for splits and that the headlining is not ripped – replacement is a specialist job.

When you drive the car, if there is a lot of trim noise, it suggests it has been taken apart for some reason.

In the front compartment, check the carpets for marking or attack by either battery or brake fluids. Feel the carpet to check for moisture and that it isn't crusted from earlier dampness. The whole area should be clean and dry.

Lift out the carpet right out of the car

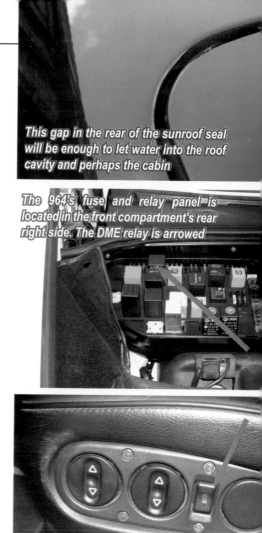

This gap in the rear of the sunroof seal will be enough to let water into the roof cavity and perhaps the cabin

The 964's fuse and relay panel is located in the front compartment's rear right side. The DME relay is arrowed

Check the electric seat adjustment and heating (if fitted) works. The heating switch is on the right

and after checking the VIN and paint code labels, ensure that the spare wheel is usable, that the toolkit is complete and that there is a jack included. The locking wheel nut socket should be present, the inflation compressor present and this should work properly on the cigarette lighter socket.

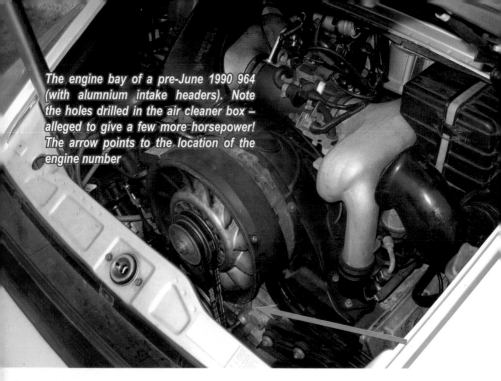

The engine bay of a pre-June 1990 964 (with alumnium intake headers). Note the holes drilled in the air cleaner box – alleged to give a few more horsepower! The arrow points to the location of the engine number

Engine

The most important aspect of any air-cooled 911 engine is that it has had regular oil and filter changes (ideally as part of a full and documented service history). It is important to see records of the annual changes, and that only a top quality oil has been used.

The oil is used for cooling as well as lubrication, so the correct level and quality is important.

On the 964, the dipstick and oil filler can be found inside the engine bay, on the right hand side. Their caps are both coloured yellow. Don't confuse the cap with that of the power steering fluid reservoir, which has a black gear-shaped cap.

To check the oil level, you can look at the combination gauge on the dash (see page 17), but you will note that the needle stays rooted to the bottom of the gauge just after the engine is started. This is because the system is a dry-sump arrangement and the level is measured in the remote oil tank (located in the right rear wing). It is important to let the engine warm fully and only check the level with the engine idling.

Pull the dipstick and look for a dark, amber-coloured fluid. If it is coloured black, then the oil needs changing. Untrained hands can also result in an overfill of oil (particularly if the level is checked when the engine is switched off). Poor servicing can result in the level dropping to a seriously low level.

If there is a mismatch between what you see on the dipstick and what the cabin gauge is registering, it is possible that the gauge may be broken, (particularly if the needle is registering empty or full).

Any condensation in the oil filler cap (in the form of creamy deposits) indicates an infrequently-used engine or one that has been used for short journeys. Either can cause long-term problems with engine wear.

With the engine idling at between 750-900rpm and the oil warm, the oil pressure should be at least 1.5 bar (22 psi) and the needle should not fluctuate. The pressure should rise to over 4 bar (60psi) from 2,500rpm.

If there is smoke from the engine when the accelerator is pressed, there is something amiss inside (valves, valve guides, etc). Some smoke on start-up is OK, as this can be caused by a small amount of oil pooling in the horizontal cylinders.

The 964 has a poor reputation for engine oil leaks. To assess the leakage situation, you have to safely get under the car and remove the fiddly M10 nuts that retain the engine undertray. This is normally a job for a specialist.

Oil can escape the 964 engine past incorrectly-seated crankcase through bolts. Normally it's the left side of the engine that is affected, with oil appearing to cover the cylinder/crankcase area.

Leaking cylinder heads will show oil from the tops of the cylinders. The cylinder head gaskets were introduced during the 1991 model year from engine numbers 62M06836 (manual gearbox) or 62M52757 (automatic gearbox). The photo shows the location of the engine number.

The vulnerable oil pipes are those entering the front right of the crankcase (difficult to see as there is a piece of engine sheet metal preventing view form the rear) and the long pipe that runs in front of the silencer.

It's an expensive job to have either the through-bolts or cylider heads fixed (both

The rear seating can accommodate two young teenage children, but adults are a squeeze for anything other than short runs

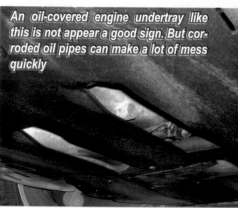
An oil-covered engine undertray like this is not appear a good sign. But corroded oil pipes can make a lot of mess quickly

The most difficult – and corrosion prone – pipe to get at with the engine in the car is at the front right side of the crankcase. This has been recently replaced

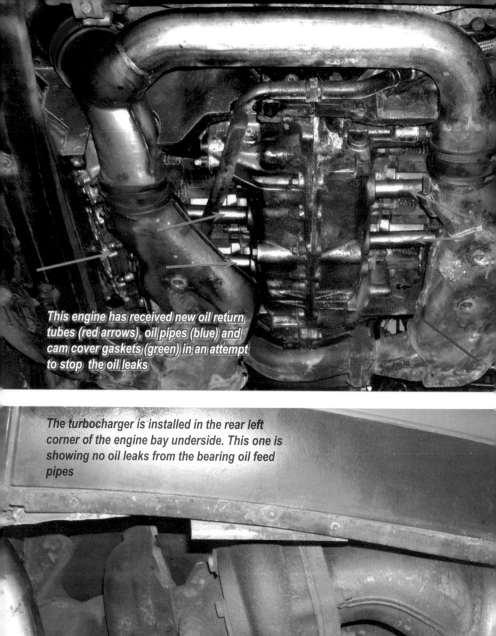

This engine has received new oil return tubes (red arrows), oil pipes (blue) and cam cover gaskets (green) in an attempt to stop the oil leaks

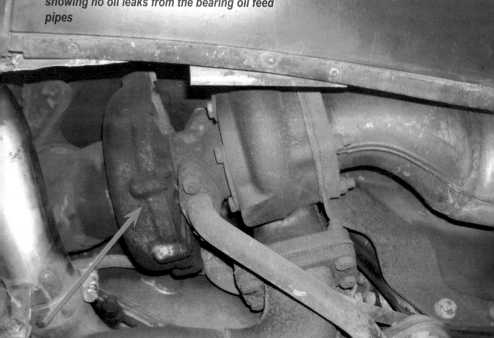

The turbocharger is installed in the rear left corner of the engine bay underside. This one is showing no oil leaks from the bearing oil feed pipes

require a minimum top end engine rebuild).

When it comes to leaks, don't get over-enthusiastic in the search for a bone-dry engine. A little oil sweat is no problem to live with, particularly from areas such as the cam cover gaskets. Oil leaks by themselves do not (normally) cause the engine to run badly (but it is important to check the oil level regularly).

A well-serviced 964 engine should run at least 120,000 miles (190,000km) before needing a cylinder head overhaul.

The engine electrical system depends on good integrity of the connections between the Bosch Motronic control unit and the ignition and fuel injection. It isn't always easy to identify faults in this area and for servicing, the right diagnostic equipment is essential. If the engine doesn't start at all, the first thing to check is the DME relay (found on the fuse panel). This is a low-cost replacement.

The only other potential weak link in the ignition system is the double distributor arrangement. On the early 964s, this system developed a reputation for consuming the small toothed belt that drives the upper distributor. The problem was that the belt was hardening (and so breaking) in the ozone-rich air inside the distributor casings. From the 1992 models, a breather was fitted to the base of the top distributor and its plastic pipe runs to the inlet ducting. Most earlier 964s will have had this retrofitted. Check the pipe is securely in place. The toothed belt should be replaced every 50,000 miles (80,000km).

Finally, check the integrity of the heat exchangers and silencer. The underbody panels will make access to these difficult, but it is important to check that there are no unexpected corrosion or damage problems. Some cars will also have by-pass pipes fitted in place of the catalytic converter (on the left side of the engine) or they will have a sports silencer. This is a

The RS engine bay doesn't look any different from a regular Carrera 2, but note the solid bushes for the engine mounting hanger (arrowed) and the single V-belt to the fan. Compare this bay with those on page 22

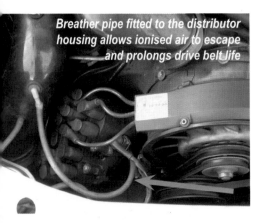

Breather pipe fitted to the distributor housing allows ionised air to escape and prolongs drive belt life

Corroded oil return tube on a Turbo will need replacement soon. The lower one has already been changed

Bolt head showing on the flywheel of this Carrera 2 suggests it is the Freudenberg type

matter of personal choice, but in some locations, the exhaust emissions and noise levels may be unacceptable.

The important point to check with the RS engine is that the engine number comes from the correct series. Otherwise, problems are relatively few. These engines were selected from the general 964 production and although they suffer from oil pipe corrosion and some instances of through-bolt leakage, the main problem is wear and tear and the extent of modification.

Worn valve guides show themselves with smoke on hard acceleration, while a heavily modified intake or exhaust system (for extra power) can reduce the value of the car.

The Turbo's 3.3-litre engine is the tried and tested 930 unit carried over from the earlier model and doesn't suffer from the same oil leak problems as the 3.6-litre M64 engine. Check underneath for corroded engine parts, including oil return pipes (the large diameter pipes between the heads and the crankcase), leaky oil feed pipes to the turbocharger (located on the rear left side of the engine), and generally, worn crankshaft or cylinder head seals.

There should be no smoke under hard acceleration (which may suggest a worn turbo) and the boost gauge should read a maximum of 0.7bar (10psi).

Transmission
The 964 has the Getrag G50 5-speed manual gearbox. This has proven to be a robust unit and although developing a 'looser' feel as the mileage goes beyond 120,000 miles (and assuming the oil has been changed at the correct intervals), it should be nonetheless trouble-free.

When driving the car, make a point of going up and down through all the gears. Fixing problems in the G50 can be expensive, although reconditioned units are an option.

The 1989 964s had a conventional flywheel, but from the start of the 1990 model year a dual-mass flywheel was fitted to reduce vibration in the drivetrain (on both C4 and C2). The rubber damped units were made by the Freudenberg company and their aim was to provide the smooth running of a large flywheel, without compromising the acceleration response. Unfortunately, these developed a reputation for failure. The symptom is a pronounced vibration and rattling during acceleration.

For the 1992 C2 models, a new dual-mass flywheel, manufactured by LUK, replaced the earlier item and the problem was largely solved. The C4 was given a modified Freudenberg unit at this point. The Turbo was also fitted with a modified Freudenberg unit. Many earlier C2s and C4s have since been fitted with the LUK flywheel. If you can get safe access under the car, identify the LUK unit by its welded-on starter ring gear (the Freudenberg has a bolted-on gear).

These problems didn't affect the RS, as this was fitted with a conventional single-mass flywheel.

A typical 964 clutch should last 50-70,000 miles, although it strongly depends on the usage profile. Accelerate from walking speed in second gear and there should be no slip or judder in the drive.

All Turbo models came with a standard limited slip differential. The condition of the friction plates is found by reversing around a tight corner. There should be a noticeable 'chirping' sound from the plates.

The Tiptronic shift gate offers two modes of two-pedal driving. With the lever on the left side of the gate (right), there is a conventional P-R-N-D-3-2-1 shift.

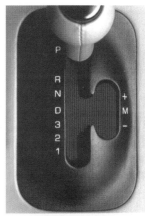

If the lever is moved to the right side, (middle) gears can be shifted by 'tipping' the lever backwards or forwards. In this mode, gears can also be shifted by the buttons on the steering wheel (lower).

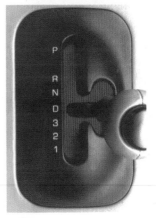

The gearbox and torque converter have a good reliability record, but check all the operation modes and that there's no jerkiness in the shift. Underneath there shouldn't be oil leaks or other signs of damage

Suspension and steering

After accident damage to the lower control arms, the main symptom of tired suspension on the 964 is worn bushes. This will reveal itself in the steering as a slight randomness, as if the car is tramlining.

With the front wheels off the ground, this may be detectable by rocking the wheels about a longitudinal axis (with the hands at the top and bottom of the wheel). This will also reveal any wheel bearing or steering rack wear.

At the rear, the main problem is again suspension joint wear. This is revealed

Check the brake flexis (red arrow) and all the drive shaft boots (green) for perishing and splits

Check the brake discs for overall wear . If there is a rim at the edge greater than 1.5mm, then its probably ready for replacement

on the move by random knocking sounds from beneath the car. Underneath, examine the anti-roll bar joints (the rubberised bushes wear or harden) and check that the boots around the driveshafts are not split. If they are, new constant velocity joints may be required. A constant whine from the wheels when driving can confirm worn constant velocity joints or wheel bearings .

The dampers shouldn't have any leaks – if they have they must be replaced.

Some owners may have fitted harder springs (with reduced ride height) and shock absorbers. By themselves, such modifications are not bad, but you should satisfy yourself that you like the ride and more importantly, whether the car has been used extensively for track days.

The RS models have hard-mounted dampers, using aluminium 'Uniball' top mountings. The aluminium bushes are easily visible in both the front and rear compartments.

Brakes, wheels and tyres

Tyres are illegal in the UK if any part of the tread area is less than 1.6mm. On a car such as the 964, where stopping from high speed in the wet is a distinct possibility, it is advised that the tyres are changed long before the wear reaches this stage. There should also be no uneven wear across the tread area – if there is it suggests there is steering or suspension misalignment.

Look for quality 'ZR' rated tyres and don't underestimate the replacement cost. These should be only from the recognised brand names, such as Pirelli, Michelin, Continental, Bridgestone or Yokohama.

All 964s came with alloy wheels. The standard Carrera fit is a 17-inch rim. The first cars had the easy-to-clean 7-spoke disc type and 1992-on models the Cup Design 91 alloys. The Carrera RS comes with special magnesium alloy Cup design wheels, which are embossed with 'Magnesium' and 'Made by SM' wording on the rims.

Only the later 3.3-litre Turbo S, Turbo 3.6 and RS 3.8 models were fitted with 18-inch rims. Generally, Cup Design alloys are the most desirable fit on any Carrera.

Non-standard or customised wheels (particularly wheels of a different design) very rarely add anything to the resale value of a car. Always try to get the seller to include the originals as part of the purchase.

A good set of wheels can make or break a car's desirability. If the wheels are scratched, chipped (by tyre fitters) or have excessive aluminium corrosion (particularly on the inner area of the rim, behind the spokes), then the car will be worth less.

Refurbishment of paint-chipped wheels is straightforward, but you only get what you pay for. Kerbing damage to the rim can point also to wheel alignment problems.

The service records should show that the brake fluid has been changed in the past two years. The pedal should be relatively light and it will pull the car up firmly without having to use excessive foot pressure. Poorly-maintained brakes can also pull the car to one side when you press the pedal.

You can check the caliper brake pad condition using a small torch, either looking through the holes in the wheels or from under the car. The brake pad wear indicator will light up on the dash when the pads get down to about 2mm, but if you don't want to replace the little senders (that insert into the pads), it pays to replace the pads before this point. If the brakes squeal when the pedal is pressed, it suggests the caliper backing plates are worn and should be replaced. If the caliper turns out to be corroded and the plates cannot be removed, replacement of the whole unit is the only solution.

The discs should not be worn more than 1.5mm on either face and these should be perfectly smooth. You can check this with a tyre tread depth indicator. Rust build-up isn't normally a problem on 964 discs.

Cross-drilled discs (found on the RS, Turbo and Turbo-look models) will need changing if there are cracks visible between the drillings or if there is circumferential grooving on the disc face.

The first generation ABS fitted to the 964 has had some problems. If the warning light remains on after starting, it means the system has a fault and has been disabled (although the brakes will continue to work satisfactorily). ABS problems have been traced to broken wheel speed sensors or worse, the ABS control unit.

Finally always check the tools and emergency wheel equipment is present.

Check it's all there! A full toolkit, compressor, jack and emergency wheel

What to look for – at a glance

Glass
Check the headlamp and turn s[...] lenses for chips and cracks. [...] windscreen should only have minor pi[...] chips – anything larger looks unsightl[...] may compromise driving safety

Documents
Check the VIN to prove the car is what it claims to be. There should be a regular service history and ideally, bills or annual roadworthiness slips to support a low mileage car. Oil changes should be annual if mileage is low.

Frontal area
Check all the frontal panels, including the polyurethane bumper and under the headlamps for stone chips and uneven panel gaps. Check under the bumper for any signs of hard grounding

Front compartment
Take out the carpeting and check the VIN on the tab under the gasoline tank. Check the same number on the VIN plate (on the right inner wing) and check the colour code label is in place beside it. Check there is no obvious damage repairs, no battery acid or brake fluid leakage

Tyres
Check that quality VR or ZR ra[...] tyres with adequate tread d[...] (no less than 1.6mm in the [...] are fitted all round. Misalignm[...] or wrong inflation pressure [...] cause uneven wear

omising

64 is the most suited of any 911 to tasteful
mising. 'Teardrop' mirrors, clear front turn
lenses and side repeaters, and the later
Design alloys add value and desirability to
rly car

Cabriolet roofs

Check the operation is smooth and closes
properly on to the windscreen rim. Check
the material seams for mould and any tears
or other damage. The plastic rear window should be crystal clear and not split,
heavily scratched or fogged

Engine oil

Check the oil level and quality
when the engine is idling and fully
warmed. The level can be seen
also on the combi gauge on the
dash panel.

Upper body

Check the whole of the upper body for
overspray (indicating poor repairs), dents
and scratches. Open both doors and
close them to check fit. If the sill trim seals
have large gaps, then look closely at the
underbody sill areas, jack points and lower
panels for signs of poor repairs

Engine

Check underbody for excessive oil leaks and
bills to ensure the later dual-mass flywheel
and head gaskets (if appropriate) have been
installed

Transmission

Check clutch for slip or judder and any bills
for evidence of a recent clutch change. On
Tiptronics, check all the operating modes and
that the shift is smooth

els

s are likely to have been refurbished, but check
erious chips, inner rim corrosion and scrapes
e rims. Nearly all scrapes can be repaired
pt bent rims), but don't under-estimate the

About the author

Peter Morgan has a Bachelors degree in Mechanical Engineering and trained in the automotive industry. He has written for publication since his teens and became Technical Editor of Porsche Post (the magazine of the Porsche Club Great Britain) in 1981. He was Editor from 1991 to 1994. His first Porsche book, Porsche 911 -- Purchase and DIY Restoration was published in 1987. To date, he has written 20 titles on all aspects of Porsche, including racing, and his books have been translated into seven languages.

As a professional journalist, he is a member of the Guild of Motoring Writers and contributes to mainstream motoring magazines worldwide. He offers a personal independent pre-purchase consultancy for Porsche drivers. For more information, go to www.petermorgan.org.uk

Acknowledgements

To Porsche AG for the use of the 964 press photographs used in this text. To Porsche Cars Great Britain, Porsche Cars North America for their help in supplying market-specific data. All other photographs are supplied by Peter Morgan Media Ltd.

Ultimate Buyers Guides include:

Porsche 911 The Classics (1964 to 1989)
ISBN 978 0 9549990 9 4 (Feb 08)
Porsche 911SC 1977 to 1983
ISBN 0 9545579 0 5
Porsche 911 Carrera 3.2 1983 to 1989;
ISBN 0 9545579 1 3
Porsche 911 Carrera, Turbo & RS (964)
ISBN 978 09549990 4 9 (2nd edition)
Porsche 911 Carrera, RS & Turbo (993);
ISBN 978 09549990 1 8 (2nd edition)
Porsche Boxster & Cayman
All models 1996 to 2007;
ISBN 978 09549990 6 3 (3rd edition)
Porsche 911 Carrera, Turbo & GT (996)
ISBN 978 09549990 7 X (2nd edition)
MGF and TF
ISBN 0 9545579 6 4
Land Rover Discovery
ISBN 0 9545579 7 2
Subaru Impreza
ISBN 09545579 8 0

And watch out for new titles!